PHOTOCOPY PERMISSION

The right to photocopy material in *Bible Journeys Holiday Club* is granted fo
photocopying clause, 'Reproduced with permission from *Bible Journeys Holiday*
(978 1 84101 808 9)', so long as reproduction is for use in a teaching situation by the original purchaser.
The right to photocopy material is not granted for anyone other than the original purchaser without written
permission from BRF.

THE COPYRIGHT LICENSING AGENCY (CLA)

If you are resident in the UK and you have a photocopying licence with the Copyright Licensing Agency (CLA),
please check the terms of your licence. If your photocopying request falls within the terms of your licence, you
may proceed without seeking further permission. If your request exceeds the terms of your CLA licence, please
contact the CLA direct with your request. Copyright Licensing Agency, 90 Tottenham Court Road, London W1T
4LP. Telephone 020 7631 5555; fax 020 7631 5500; email cla@cla.co.uk; website www.cla.co.uk. The CLA will
provide photocopying authorisation and royalty fee information on behalf of BRF.

BRF is a Registered Charity (No. 233280)

Text copyright © Eleanor Zuercher 2006, 2011
Illustrations copyright © Paula Doherty 2006
The author asserts the moral right
to be identified as the author of this work

Published by
The Bible Reading Fellowship
15 The Chambers, Vineyard
Abingdon OX14 3FE
United Kingdom
Tel: +44 (0)1865 319700
Email: enquiries@brf.org.uk
Website: www.brf.org.uk
BRF is a Registered Charity

ISBN 978 1 84101 808 9
First published 2011
10 9 8 7 6 5 4 3 2 1 0

Acknowledgments
Unless otherwise stated, scripture quotations are taken from the Contemporary English Version of the Bible published by HarperCollins Publishers, copyright © 1991, 1992, 1995 American Bible Society.

Scripture quotations taken from the Holy Bible, New International Version, copyright © 1973, 1978, 1984, 1995 by International Bible Society, are used by permission of Hodder & Stoughton Publishers, a member of the Hachette Livre UK Group. All rights reserved. 'NIV' is a registered trademark of International Bible Society. UK trademark number 1448790.

Scriptures quoted from the Good News Bible published by The Bible Societies/HarperCollins Publishers Ltd, UK © American Bible Society 1966, 1971, 1976, 1992, used with permission.

A catalogue record for this book is available from the British Library

Printed in Singapore by Craft Print International Ltd

BIBLE JOURNEYS HOLIDAY CLUB

A five-day holiday club plan
for small churches

Eleanor Zuercher

Eleanor Zuercher is a trained primary teacher and experienced children's work leader. For many years she lived and worked in a rural parish in the West Buckingham Benefice (a group of six rural parishes), where she ran workshops for children aged 3–12. Alongside this work, she oversaw all the children's work for her parish as well as being involved in planning and taking services. Eleanor is married with a young family. She is author of *Not Sunday, Not School!* (Barnabas, 2006) and *Through the Year with Jesus!* (Barnabas, 2009).

For my good friend Claire and her son, Dominic

Acknowledgments

With grateful thanks to Sue Doggett, my editor, who has done so much work in preparation for this book, and without whom it would not have been published at all. Thanks are also owed to the children and parents in the West Buckingham Benefice who allowed me to try out my ideas on them.

The material in this book was first published in *Not Sunday, Not School!* (Barnabas, 2006). The sessions are presented as a series to provide a five-day holiday club programme for those working in rural areas with small groups of children, but individual sessions could also be used as stand-alone activity days. The theme of journeys fits well with the end of the school year, when many of the children might be travelling to go on holiday. There are plenty of journeys in the Bible to tell the children about!

CONTENTS

HOW TO USE THIS BOOK

This book contains a five-session thematic holiday club programme for small churches, designed not only to assist with integrating the children's work into the life of the rural church, but also to help integrate the regular congregation into the children's work.

The sessions are planned with flexible timings so that activities can be lengthened or shortened depending on the age of the children, their ability to concentrate, and how much they like the type of activity on offer. There are suggestions in the session plans (see pages 38–42) for running activities simultaneously by splitting the children into two or three groups and rotating from one activity to the next. This could be helpful if time and space round the tables is restricted.

Each session contains:

• Suggestions for Bible stories based on the theme
• Suggestions for creating a display for the church
• Suggestions for songs
• Craft activities
• Games
• Suggestions for prayer

Because the material has been developed in the context of the rural church, the ideas and perceptions are from a rural perspective and rooted in particular challenges found in rural situations. However, the entirety of this experience is not unique to rural churches and many of the circumstances encountered would equally apply in the urban context. The hope is that the material will encourage children's leaders in smaller churches to run holiday clubs with few resources. With a bit of lateral and creative thinking, perceived weaknesses can become strengths and the end result will be that a holiday club, even in a small church, can become vibrant and successful.

OPPORTUNITIES AND ADVANTAGES

The challenge of working with a small number of children provides an ideal opportunity for encouragement and reward. For example, small numbers mean that you will be able to get to know and serve individual children far better. Also, you will have the advantage of being able to tailor your holiday club to your own individual requirements.

Use your holiday club session times productively by keeping the teaching focused. Rather than coming to church on a regular basis, some children may only attend the holiday club, so this will be a golden opportunity to enjoy telling the children Bible stories that they might not otherwise hear, especially some of the Old Testament stories.

TIMING OF THE ACTIVITIES

Each activity is designed to last between 10 and 15 minutes. Sample plans for each session, showing an outline programme for younger and older children, can be found on pages 38–42.

The suggested activities for creating a display for the church are designed to last between 15 and 20 minutes. However, depending on the age and ability of the children, more time can be spent on them as required. Creating a display for the church is an ideal way to make the holiday club visible to those in the wider congregation who are not involved, as well as providing an enjoyable and memorable record of the event.

ADDITIONAL MATERIAL

Extra ideas for integrating children's work into the wider congregation beyond the holiday club itself can be found on the website www.barnabasinchurches. org.uk/nsns.

INTRODUCTION

In order to ensure that your holiday club runs as smoothly as possible, you will need to think carefully about your situation and how to work with or around any potential difficulties. Decisions about where the event will take place, the best time to hold it, and who is going to be involved, are all vital.

Venue

When choosing a venue, there may be a number of options, such as a village hall or school hall. However, you are likely to need to hire these venues, which can be expensive. As an alternative, you might like to consider using your church building. It is likely that the use of the building will be free, and you are more likely to be able to make arrangements to store materials in situ for the duration of the holiday club. Also, the richness of resources for Christian teaching and the subconscious osmosis of the wealth of symbols employed in a church are excellent.

However, the main problem with using the church building, particularly in a very old church, will be the lack of modern facilities. It is essential that the building can be heated sufficiently, particularly if the holiday club is planned to run early or late in the year. You will also need light (natural or artificial) so that the children can see to do any craft activities. With regard to toilet facilities, if one of your group's leaders (or perhaps another member of the congregation) lives close enough, it may be possible to arrange for the children to use their facilities. For child protection reasons, you will need to draw up procedures for this (discussed on pages 8–9). Alternatively, you may be able to arrange the hire of portable toilets for the duration of the holiday club.

Many old churches lack kitchen facilities and you may need to arrange your planning accordingly. For example, it is likely to be impractical for the children to cook anything very elaborate, although simple things such as the ideas in the 'Food for the journey' activity (p. 30) can work well. You will need to provide cold storage for the food before and after preparation (cool boxes will be suitable if a fridge is not available), and the means for the children to wash their hands before and after handling food.

Timing

Deciding which days to hold the holiday club and for how long it should run will depend on a number of local factors. With regard to the number of sessions, it is best to be realistic about your abilities. Running a two-hour holiday club programme is very intensive while the session is in progress. Running this type of activity every day for a whole week would certainly be very hard work and will also consume time and mental energy in terms of planning and preparation. Smaller, shorter sessions held for just two or three days may be more manageable.

Alternatively, you may wish to consider running the holiday club over two and a half days. This programme would include a two-hour session in the morning and again in the afternoon, plus a short break for lunch, on the first two days, and then a further two-hour morning session on the third day. The children will need to bring a packed lunch for the midday break on Days 1 and 2. If the final morning session is followed by a short act of worship, the time on that day will be extended by up to half an hour. However, a special multi-age service to conclude the event could be run on the Sunday following the holiday club event (see page 13 for a service outline). Parents, carers and church members not involved in the holiday club could be invited to come along and join in the celebration.

The length of each session is important. The model used in this book is for each session to last for two hours, but, when deciding on this point, you need to think about how the children will be arriving. If parents will be driving them—perhaps from other villages some miles away—it is a good idea to make sure the parents will have enough time to go and do something else, or to go back home and have more than a ten-minute cup of tea before turning round and driving back to collect their children. In other words, the sessions need to be long enough to make it worthwhile for the parents as well.

Publicity

Telling people about the holiday club you propose to run is important. Putting up posters and sending out invitations are good ways to make sure people know that the holiday club is taking place. Make sure the event is advertised in your church magazine or newsletter and announced at services. Make sure that baptism families and parents and carers attending Christian basics courses, such as Alpha, are told about the children's work and receive invitations too. You can also advertise the event in your local schools, but you may need to cap the numbers so that you are not overwhelmed with children. The most important publicity will be by word of mouth, so your holiday club is likely to grow in popularity if it is run at the same time each year for a number of consecutive years. Children will tell their friends, and their parents will tell their friends.

Funding

Don't worry if you don't have a limitless expenses fund and all the state-of-the-art technology you could want. Concentrate instead on making your holiday club imaginative, creative and unique. The enjoyment the children get out of your sessions will not depend on technology—that is only a means to an end. Also, if you are lacking a nicely furnished, carpeted, warm room, make sure you use the symbolism, images and atmosphere that are readily available in the building you do use—especially if it is the church. The church building is entirely different from any other place that many of the children are likely to go into on a regular basis. The children will appreciate that it is special, particularly if you make their time there special too.

You will, of course, need some financial support for your holiday club. You may find that there are trust funds available or your PCC or governing council may allow you a budget. Unless absolutely necessary, it is best not to charge admission for children to attend. It is essential that any child who wishes to come should be able to do so. In addition, it is not recommended that any collection should be taken at a concluding act of worship. If parents and carers wish to make a donation, provision should be made for them to do so, but there should be no expectations about this.

You might like to consider raising funds for a named charity to which the children wish to give, but, equally, a general fundraising effort, perhaps by the church council, would be helpful if funds are required for the running of the holiday club itself. Ideas for fundraising can be found on the website: www.barnabasinchurches.org.uk/nsns.

With forward planning, many of the items needed for crafts, games and displays can be requested well ahead of the event, and donation boxes for items can be set out in the church to collect contributions from the congregation.

CHILD PROTECTION AND HEALTH AND SAFETY

It is essential that you give both child protection and health and safety considerable attention. Your diocese, governing body or equivalent should be able to provide you with up-to-date detailed information about what is required and how to go about fulfilling the requirements. It is vital that all your helpers are registered with the Independent Safeguarding Authority (ISA) and have an enhanced certificate of disclosure from the Criminal Records Bureau (CRB), and that you comply with the law by making sure your holiday club is run with proper attention to child protection and health and safety. Remember that the safeguards are there to protect not only the children who are in your care but also the young leaders and adult helpers. Where you need assistance, ask for it.

Obtaining clearance and holding records can easily be done by someone who wishes to support your children's work but may not be able to offer any physical help.

Child protection

Make sure you know how a child's disclosure of neglect or abuse at home should be handled. Check this with your diocese or equivalent. You are likely to find that there is someone nominated by the diocese or your church's governing body to deal with these issues, which will avoid the situation (particularly destructive in close-knit communities) of neighbours being told, or perhaps the minister becoming aware of too much detail, which will make his or her continuing ministry to the family difficult. You may think that this scenario is unlikely in a small community where everyone appears to know everyone else's business, but we can never be sure what goes on behind closed doors. Waiting until after a disclosure has been made before finding out how it should have been handled is too late.

Check the requirements for the ratio of adults to children at your sessions. This will depend on the age of the children present, but in any case you should always have enough adults to ensure that there are at least two present at any time with any child. Allow for the possibility of one adult having to leave the room for some reason: there should always be two left behind.

First aid

At least one adult assisting with the holiday club should be a qualified first aider. If you need more people to be qualified, find out about local training courses for child first aid.

Registration

Make sure you have documentation giving certain minimum information about the children in your care. A simple registration form will be sufficient for this. It should give the name and date of birth of the child, contact details including emergency contact details, information about any allergies and the name of the child's doctor. Permission for things like administration of first aid and taking of photographs could also be included. A draft example can be found on page 35, or downloaded from the website www. barnabasinchurches.org.uk/nsns.

Also, you will need to register each child as they arrive so that you have a daily record of attendance. In this way, you will be able to keep track of those children who do not normally attend your church and follow up those who have not attended for a period of time. (See page 34 for a sample registration form.) As you register each child, write his or her name on a simple badge made from a self-adhesive label. Alternatively, if the children have prebooked their places, you could preprint badges with the children's names (have blanks available for last-minute bookings). You could make the badges in footprint shapes to match the journeying theme or choose a simple fish shape as a sign that it is a Christian holiday club.

A signing in and signing out form for parents as they drop off and collect children will ensure that you know which children are present at the holiday club. The form should also have space for a parent to notify you if someone else will be collecting their child. A sample form is provided on page 36, or can be downloaded from the website www. barnabasinchurches.org.uk/nsns.

Health and safety

Check with your PCC or governing council that you have appropriate insurance cover. You should ensure that the electrical checks on wiring and equipment, and the fire extinguisher checks, are up to date. Make sure you know where the fire escape exits are, and that they can be easily accessed in the event of fire. Doors may need to be watched, however, to ensure that children don't escape during the holiday club sessions.

Remember that children can get noisy and carried away by the excitement of the moment. Investing in a bell or other method of making an even louder noise to get their attention is very worthwhile and saves untold damage to the vocal chords.

Carry out a risk assessment by viewing the building or room(s) you will be using, from a child's point of view. If you are using an old church, be aware of hard and possibly steep stone steps, unguarded heaters, things that are shouting out to be climbed, or other hazards. Such hazards may not preclude the use of the building but some will need to be dealt with, for example, by placing secure guards around heaters and designating certain areas as out-of-bounds. No room can ever be completely safe, but you must take every precaution to ensure the safety of the children in your care.

THE SESSIONS

The session plans are presented as a series for a five-day holiday club. However, they were conceived and tested as individual sessions, so they will work equally well if you wish to hold the holiday club over fewer days, or even for whole-day events.

The holiday club can be expanded or contracted, depending on the number of children attending. For example, to expand, the learning of a song could easily be inserted. Also, it makes sense to have smaller groups of children doing different activities at the same time. For example, if you have three activities running before a break, and there are twelve children in the group, it would make sense to divide them into three groups of four and run each activity three times concurrently, so the children circulate between activities. You do need extra helpers for this, but it is well worthwhile for the extra attention you can give to each child. In addition, when considering the order of activities, do bear in mind that if you want displays to be ready before the children leave, any paint or glue will need time to dry. Any work that the children are taking home will also be much easier to carry if it isn't too wet.

You are likely to find that the number of different activities you need to keep children occupied and involved will vary greatly. This will depend partly on the age of the children. Most nine-year-olds can stick at an activity and will wish to do so for longer than a four-year-old. The nine-year-old will be more meticulous and will get bored less quickly; so older children tend to need fewer activities to fill a two-hour session. That said, some activities, even for younger children, will engross them more than you might have anticipated, so you may find you are running out of time. You will need to be flexible and have a strategy for cutting activities if, halfway through the session, it looks as if there will not be time for everything. Although this may mean wasted preparation, materials can always be used in future sessions, and it is much better to have too much than to be floundering around trying to fill the last half-hour because you have too little.

Some of the activities suggested involve a certain amount of time in preparation. For a few (but not all, by any means), certain more expensive materials might be required. If these are too expensive, there are plenty of other activities to choose from—although you may find that spending a little extra money for the special occasion of a once-a-year holiday club is worth it. Children can tell when the materials you offer them are sub-standard; they can also tell when time and trouble have been put into the activities on offer, and will respond positively. If an activity is worth doing, it is worth doing properly. Even if, for example, 90 stars need to be cut out of card for one of the activities, if the work is divided among a sufficient number of helpers, the burden is considerably reduced.

You will also need to consider how to deal with the inevitable messiness resulting from craft activities. Tables may need to be covered with newspaper or, better still, plastic-covered fabric cut to size, which can simply be wiped clean after the session. You will need kitchen towel or wipes for some activities, and hand-washing equipment.

It is also a good idea to provide something to occupy children who finish an activity ahead of time.

Ideas include a whiteboard or blackboard to doodle on, some construction toys, or books.

You may also want to consider setting up a quiet corner with beanbags, books and colouring materials, so that children can take time out if they need to. This area can also be used as a prayer zone. The area should be in a quiet place but not isolated. Children using it should be visible at all times and accompanied by at least two adult helpers who have been given the task of supervising the area. Objects or pictures related to the journeys theme could be placed here to encourage the children to explore the theme independently; or you might wish to use feely boxes, filled with items relating to the theme for the day (see pages 50–51 for instructions).

Telling stories

There are a number of low-tech but very effective ways to tell stories. If you are just going to read the story (and there is nothing wrong with that), it is a good idea to practise beforehand, or even try it out on another person. Make sure you understand the flow of the story so that you can read it well without getting caught out by unusual punctuation. If you are reading from the Bible, read a few versions and pick the one that the children will understand best. If there are pictures, use them and make sure the children can see them. Make sure you read clearly and slowly enough for everyone to hear and understand.

It is a good idea to get some variety in to your storytelling which will make it easier to keep the children's attention. Some suggestions are outlined below, all of which are achievable without too great an expense. The list is not exhaustive!

Creative storytelling using visual aids

Using visual aids to tell stories works fantastically well. The story can be told in simple language, using slow deliberate movements in the placing of figures, objects and artefacts on a base cloth. The effect of this is that the story itself and not the storyteller becomes the main focus of attention. The children are typically very calm and become drawn in by the story, although adult helpers are needed to sit with them in order to deal with any cases of restlessness or interruptions and so allow the storyteller to maintain concentration. For more information about creative storytelling using this method, visit www.godlyplay.co.uk.

Performance storytelling

At the other end of the spectrum, you might like simply to learn the Bible passage and recite it from heart instead of reading it. This way, the storyteller removes the book, which can act as a barrier between the teller and the hearers, maintaining constant eye contact with the hearers and concentrating on putting life into the story. Hearing the Bible in this way can be enthralling. However, if you find it too difficult to learn the passage word for word, once you are familiar enough with it you could always retell the story in your own words instead.

You could also experiment with dramatic readings, requiring two or more people to read the story. *The Dramatised Bible* is an excellent resource if you don't wish to create your own scripts.

Interactive storytelling

There are several techniques you can employ to make your storytelling interactive.

- Consider using sound effects at appropriate parts of the story. Sound effects work best if you are telling the story from memory. However, don't overdo loud 'sit-up-and-take-notice' effects, as these might frighten smaller or more timid children.
- Using audience participation is also very effective. Ask the children to make a noise, or shout a word, or do an action whenever you say a particular word. Then work your way through the story with the children supplying the sound effects. You may need to edit the original text slightly to increase the frequency of the words to which they are responding.
- If you're using a repetitive story, ask the children to say a response. For example, if you are telling the creation story, prepare a large smiling face drawn on a large circle of card and ask the children to say 'it is good' every time you hold it up.
- Using objects can also be effective. In a small group, you could use feely boxes, so that the children have to guess what the items are. Use objects that are visible to everyone and either line them up as the story unfolds or give them to the children to hold while the story is in progress.
- Tell a story accurately; then, after an interval when the children have done other things, tell it again, but make it full of mistakes and see how many they

can spot. Make some of the mistakes deliberately funny and some of them less easy to spot. Children love pointing out mistakes adults make, so let them enjoy it!
- If you are able to be slightly more 'high-tech', show the children a short clip of a video related to the theme. This can be very effective, particularly if you don't use video very often in your group.

General activities

Activities such as painting, drawing, modelling using junk, clay or playdough, cutting and sticking, singing and so on, can all be used to illustrate the journeying theme. If you wish to expand some of the ideas set out in the book, you will find basic recipes on pages 46–47 and basic craft skills on pages 50–51. If your church doesn't have kitchen facilities, it may be possible to ask a member of the congregation living nearby to let you use their oven. This way, the children can even make biscuits or bread, which can be taken out of the building for baking and brought back later.

Song suggestions

General songs which could be used with any of the holiday club sessions include the following.

- Abba, Father (*Hymns Old and New* 5)
- O when the saints go marching in (*Junior Praise* 195)
- One more step along the world I go (*Hymns Old and New* 405)
- Seek ye first the kingdom of God (*Hymns Old and New* 442)
- Spirit of the living God (*Hymns Old and New* 454)
- The Lord's my shepherd (*Hymns Old and New* 490)
- The Spirit lives to set us free (*Hymns Old and New* 494)
- We are on the Lord's road (*Sing Glory* 138)
- Will you come and follow me? (*Hymns Old and New* 560)

CONCLUDING THE HOLIDAY CLUB

It is a good idea to conclude your holiday club with an act of worship to which parents, carers and members of the wider congregation are invited and welcomed. It is important that there is good support from the adult congregation for the holiday club and that the act of worship is not seen as 'just for the children'.

You can make the final act of worship relevant to the holiday club experience by using some of the things the children have been doing. For example, the children's work can be on display and, if they have been learning a song, they could teach it to the adults. Similarly, if they have written some prayers or ideas for prayers, you could read these out or ask the children to do so. Also, you could briefly recap the stories on which the holiday club has been based to give an overview of the theme, or perhaps the children could prepare a presentation of the overall theme.

During the holiday club, the children are learning by doing and having fun, mixed with a little bit of listening. A final act of worship is an excellent way of drawing the holiday club theme together and brings the whole event to a very satisfactory conclusion for children and adults alike.

Have fun!

Lastly, make sure you enjoy your holiday club. Your cheerfulness and enthusiasm will help the children to be cheerful and enthusiastic, too.

SUGGESTED OUTLINE FOR A CONCLUDING ACT OF WORSHIP

For the concluding act of worship, it is a good idea to introduce elements that are the same as or similar to those that happen in a main Sunday service, so that there will be something familiar in a main Sunday service if any of the families decide to come along at a later date. For example, if you regularly share the peace in your church, this is a good place to start. The children will enjoy shaking hands with everyone else. You might also consider using a form of creed and a simple form of confession.

A typical act of worship after a holiday club might include:

* Introduction
* Song (which may or may not be a Gloria song)
* Simple form of confession, or a thanksgiving, or a creed
* Recapping the stories
* Prayers led by the children (including the Lord's Prayer)
* Song
* Short presentation of children's work and holiday club stories
* Sharing the peace (usual wording)
* Song
* Grace and final blessing

This format is very flexible and can be adapted to suit your need. For example, the order might be rearranged so that a version of the Gloria is sung or the creed is said immediately after the recapping of the story.

BIBLE JOURNEYS HOLIDAY CLUB
SESSION PLANS

Session 1

NOAH'S JOURNEY

You will find the story of Noah in Genesis 6:1—9:17. The story can be told using any of the approaches outlined on pages 10–11. There are also many picture books telling the story, or you could use a children's Bible, such as *The Barnabas Children's Bible* (Barnabas, 2007).

Story synopsis

After God had made the world, he looked on his creation with joy and was glad that it was good. After a while, though, the people that he had made began to turn their backs on God and did lots of wrong things. God realised that he needed to wash everything clean and make it new again, so he decided to send a great flood to wash all the wickedness away. But there was one person who loved God. His name was Noah. Noah's family included his wife and three sons, and their wives.

God told Noah to build an ark. He told him exactly how to build it and what to use; and he told him to make sure he put two of every kind of animal into the ark, so that what was good could be saved.

As soon as the ark had been built, it began to rain and rain. It didn't stop raining for 40 days and 40 nights. As the water flooded the land, the ark began to float. Eventually, the rain stopped and the water level began to fall. Noah sent out a dove but the bird returned because there was nowhere to perch yet. The second time, the dove came back with an olive leaf; but when Noah sent out the dove for a third time, he knew when it didn't return that it had found dry land.

Noah and his family gave thanks to God for saving them, and God put a rainbow into the sky to be a sign of his promise never to send such a flood again.

DISPLAYS FOR THE CHURCH

Noah's ark display

> **Time duration: 20 minutes (pre-session preparation)**
>
> **You will need:** a large piece of cardboard or a section cut from a cardboard box, paint and brushes, animals made by the children.

Before the session, make a backdrop against which to display cardboard tube animals (see the craft activity on pages 17–18). If you have time, you could make the backdrop as an activity with the children.

SONGS FOR NOAH'S JOURNEY

There are lots of good songs about Noah that the children could learn and sing during the concluding act of worship. Suggestions include:

- Rise and shine (*Hymns Old and New* 436)
- Have you heard the raindrops? (*Hymns Old and New* 202)
- Who put the colours in the rainbow? (*Hymns Old and New* 557)

CRAFTS FOR NOAH'S JOURNEY

Cork boats

> **Time duration: 15 minutes**
>
> **You will need:** corks (four per child), plastic drinking straws, paper, pens, large seed tray (or similar) for water, at least 75cm square, water, strong glue, Plasticine.

This is a good activity for summer when there is a chance that the children could test their boats outside (if it is raining, you can always use the tray of water inside). Before the session, lay down four corks, side by side, and glue them together to form a flat raft. Use two dots of glue for each join, leaving a gap between the dots. A hot glue gun will do the trick, although you will need to make sure the cork surfaces are grease-free so that the glue will stick. Cut the paper to size to make the sails.

Give each child a pre-glued cork raft and a straw. They will need to flatten one end of the straw and push it between the two middle corks of their raft and then use a piece of Plasticine on the underside to help keep it in place and add stability underneath the raft.

Cut two slits in the piece of paper sail so that it can be threaded on to the mast. Get each child to write their name, or otherwise decorate the sail, so that they can identify their raft. Thread the sail on to the mast.

The boats can now be tested. Put them into the dry seed tray, add water and watch the boats rising and floating on the flood. The children will be able to propel the boats across the water by blowing on the sails.

Rainbow mobiles

 Time duration: 15 minutes

You will need: white card, gold card, silver card, pair of compasses, scissors, pens, glue or sticky tape, acetate or thread.

This activity involves preparing a lot of pre-cut shapes, unless you are doing this with older children (and with enough time) for them to do their own cutting. You will need to prepare one pre-cut rainbow shape for each child. To do this, draw circles on the white card with the pair of compasses and then cut them in half, so that each circle yields two rainbows. Next, cut out sun shapes from the gold card (one for each child) and raindrop shapes from the silver card (seven for each child).

You can use thread to suspend the items from the rainbow, but you may find it quicker to use pre-cut strips of acetate to suspend the shapes. The acetate can be folded so that the raindrops seem to spray out.

Ask each child to colour in the rainbow shape in rainbow colours. If they want to follow the exact colours of the rainbow, you will probably need to remind them what they are and what order they come in (red, orange, yellow, green, blue, indigo, violet).

Use sticky tape or glue dots to attach an acetate strip to both the rainbow shape and the sun on one side and the raindrops on the other.

While you're doing this activity, talk to the children about God's promise as represented by the rainbow. You might also like to tell them how rainbows appear when sunshine and rain are mixed together, and that there is always a rainbow somewhere on earth, so God's sign can be seen somewhere on our planet at all times.

When rainbows are photographed from space, you can see that they are actually circular, without beginning or end.

BASED ON AN IDEA FROM *HERE'S ONE I MADE EARLIER* BY KATHRYN COPSEY (SCRIPTURE UNION, 1995).

Chalk pavement art

 Time duration: 15 minutes

You will need: coloured and white chalks, a paved path, black sugar paper (in case of rain).

Before undertaking this activity, make sure you have the approval of your churchwarden or whoever is in charge of the path you have chosen on which to indulge in some pavement art!

Invite the children to draw pictures to illustrate creation in chalk on the path. Take photographs of their work, but remind them that when the rain comes (as it surely will) it will wash their pictures away, just as the flood washed all of Noah's world away. When the water had gone, he wouldn't have recognised anything—no houses or villages or living things except what had been on the ark.

If it is raining, the children can do their pictures inside on black paper instead, but show them how easily chalk is brushed off.

Cardboard tube animals

 Time duration: 15 minutes

You will need: cardboard tubes (two per child), paint and brushes, glue, card, collage items such as paper, tissue paper, feathers, leather and so on, googly eyes.

Prepare the cardboard tubes: cut through each tube lengthways, then cut out a semicircle from each side of the cut edge. This will leave you with a shape like the rounded back of an animal and four 'legs'. Ease out the legs so that the animal can stand up. A head can be added in the form of a shape cut from card or foam. Give each child a pair of tubes, so they can make a pair of animals. Have a good supply of paint, card, collage items and googly eyes so that each child can turn their tube into the animal of their choice.

If you have prepared an ark scene, the animals can be displayed as part of that, or the children can take them home.

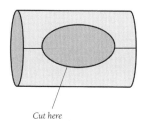 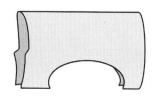

Cut here

Animal masks

 Time duration: 15 minutes

You will need: card cut into basic mask shapes, collage materials to decorate (such as paper, tissue paper, wool, feathers, leather, cotton wool, thin coloured foam and so on), glue, paint and brushes, elastic, stapler, sticky tape.

Invite each child to decorate their mask to make an animal face. When they've finished, staple the elastic to fit the child's head, making sure the staples' points are facing out. Cover the staples with sticky tape to prevent them from causing discomfort. You could use the masks at the end of the session to recap the story of Noah's ark.

Rainbow doves

 Time duration: 15 minutes

You will need: white card cut into dove shapes (see template on page 54), rainbow-coloured paper cut to size, pens.

Cut out the dove shapes and then cut a slot in the side of each one. Give each child a sheet of rainbow-coloured paper. Get them to fold the paper up in a concertina so that it is no wider than the slot. Feed the paper through the slot cut in the side of the dove and then open up the concertinas on both sides of the dove to make the wings.

The children could decorate their doves with feathers or by writing a message or drawing a picture about what the story of Noah means to them.

GAMES FOR NOAH'S JOURNEY

Racing cork boats

If the children have made cork boats, they will enjoy racing them on the tray of water or across a small, inflatable paddling pool. For safety reasons, make sure that the children know that they are not allowed to race their boats in a pool or pond.

PRAYERS FOR NOAH'S JOURNEY

Watery prayers

It seems appropriate to use water for prayers in this session. A little water could be poured into a large transparent container, such as an attractive bowl, for each prayer said. While the water is poured, thank God for his promises and all the blessings he gives us. As a second part to the prayers, the bowl could be passed round to everyone present to give them the opportunity to use the water to mark their foreheads, or the palm of their hand, in order to thank God for personal blessings and ask for his guidance on their own journeys.

Sailing prayers

With the children sitting calmly in a circle, place a tray of water in the centre of the group and use a cork boat as a focus for prayer. Set the boat off across the tray of water while a prayer is said, asking God to watch over our own life journeys.

Session 2

MOSES' JOURNEY

STORIES FOR MOSES' JOURNEY

The story of Moses' journey in this session is the story of the exodus. As this is a long story, instead of hearing everything at one sitting, you might consider breaking it into three sections (the exodus, wandering in the desert and the Ten Commandments and, finally, entering the promised land) to be told at intervals during the session. Tell the stories using any of the methods outlined on pages 10–11. Alternatively, there are Godly Play scripts for these stories (see the Bibliography on page 56). You could also use any of the stories from the time when the Israelites were wandering in the wilderness, if you wanted to.

Story synopsis

At one time, God's people were held as slaves in the land of Egypt, but God helped Moses to free the people from their slavery in Egypt and lead them to their own land, the promised land. With God's help, the people escaped from the Pharaoh of Egypt, but, when Pharaoh had stopped chasing them, they weren't sure of the right way to go.

Again God helped them by going in front of them as a thick cloud during the day, and as a flaming fire during the night. He also helped them by leaving food for them every morning, even though the people were wandering through the desert. The people were travelling in the desert for many, many years, relying on God's help, living in tents and always travelling, following Moses who was following God.

Along the way, they came to the holy mountain, Mount Sinai. The people could see that God was there because they could see fire and smoke on the mountain. They were afraid to go close, but Moses climbed the mountain to talk to God. While he was there, God told him ten rules that he wanted his people to obey to help them find the right way to live, so that they would please God.

When Moses came down the mountain, he told the people about the rules God had given. The people made a very special box. They kept the rules in the special box and carried it with them wherever they went. Later, when they reached the promised land, they put the box in a special place in the temple they built for God.

Still today, we know about the rules God gave to his people, and we try to follow them in our lives, too.

DISPLAYS FOR THE CHURCH

Road signs

 Time duration: 15 minutes

You will need: large circles and round-cornered triangles cut from red card, the same shapes but made smaller cut from white card, black paper, scissors, glue, long cardboard tubes (optional).

Talk to the children about how the Bible can show us the way to live well. Then show them a copy of the Highway Code, especially the page with road signs, and invite them to make up some road signs by cutting and sticking shapes from the black paper on to the white triangles or circles to show people how to live well (as opposed to how to drive well). The white card can then be mounted on the red to give a road-sign effect.

These signs could be fixed on cardboard tubes (such as the insides of wrapping paper) and mounted on chairs or the ends of pews for display in church.

SONGS FOR MOSES' JOURNEY

- One more step along the world I go (*Hymns Old and New* 405)
- How did Moses cross the Red Sea? (*Junior Praise* 83)
- Will you come and follow me? (*Hymns Old and New* 560)

CRAFTS FOR MOSES' JOURNEY

Compasses

 Time duration: 10 minutes

You will need: thick white card cut into circles with the centre marked, split-pin paper fasteners, compass 'needles' cut from thick white card, pens, map, a real compass.

Show the children what a compass looks like and how it works by always showing you where north is. Also show them some maps and point out that north is marked on them, too. Then give the children a pre-cut circle each and ask them to decorate the circle to create their compass. They may need help in marking the points of the compass.

Give them each a compass 'needle', also cut from card, to decorate. Fix the 'needle' to the compass base with a paper fastener.

You might like to talk to the children about what things we can use to find our way on our spiritual journey: the Bible can be a bit like a map and compass, showing us the way to God.

Packed suitcases

 Time duration: 10 minutes

You will need: thin card, pictures cut from magazines, glue, scissors.

To prepare the 'suitcases', fold a thin piece of card in half and cut out a suitcase shape so that the hinged edge is along the folded edge of the card. When you open up the 'suitcase' you have a double shape. Give one of these to each child. Ask them to pack their suitcase by choosing from the magazine pictures items that they will need on their journey. Talk about what we do and don't need and what God provides us with.

Personal arks

 Time duration: 15 minutes

You will need: small gold boxes (obtainable from craft shops or the internet), small copies of the Ten Commandments, glue, sequins, beads and so on, glitter glue, narrow ribbon.

Give each child a small gold box and a selection of sequins, glitter glue and any other (small) shiny things and ask them to decorate their boxes so that they look really special. Talk to them about how the Israelites made a special holy box called the ark of the covenant to carry the Ten Commandments with them as they travelled. When the boxes are finished, put a copy of the Ten Commandments (paraphrased from Exodus 20:3–17) into each box and tie them up with pretty ribbon.

GAMES FOR MOSES' JOURNEY

Memory game

 Time duration: 10 minutes

You will need: a tray, a cloth large enough to cover the tray, journey-related items such as a map, compass, guidebook, shoe, Bible, Highway Code, bottle of water, torch and so on.

Put the items on a tray and let the children look at them carefully. Talk about why each one is necessary, then cover them with a cloth and see how many the children can remember.

PRAYERS FOR MOSES' JOURNEY

Compass prayers

If the children have made compasses, you might like to look at them again. Ask the children what shape the points of the compass make (a cross). With each child holding their own compass, ask God to be our compass, always directing us to the right path.

Footstep prayers

Try praying while standing as a group. If you are using your church for the holiday club, you could stand in the nave. As a response to each prayer, invite everyone to take one step towards the altar end of the church, symbolising our journey to God. If you are using a hall or other space, set a cross on a table at one end of the room and invite everyone to take a step towards the cross.

Session 3

JONAH'S JOURNEY

STORIES FOR JONAH'S JOURNEY

The book of Jonah is very short, making it easy to learn and retell to the children, but there are also lots of picture-book variations on the market. The story is dramatic and works well told to the children in your own words if you have the confidence to do this.

Story synopsis

Generally speaking, the messengers God sent to his people did as God said, but there was one exception. His name was Jonah.

God said to Jonah, 'Go to Nineveh and tell the people that I know all about the awful things they do, and in 40 days Nineveh will be destroyed.'

When Jonah thought about this, he realised that, as God was a loving God, he was likely to forgive the people of Nineveh and give them a second chance. If Jonah gave them the warning and then God forgave the people, he'd end up looking silly.

So Jonah decided to run away. He went to the port of Jaffa, where he caught a boat going in the opposite direction to Nineveh. As soon as the ship was out at sea, God sent a great storm. The captain and crew were terrified and asked all the passengers to pray to their gods for safety. Jonah was fast asleep but the captain woke him and told him to pray like everyone else. Jonah realised that God was after him and explained to the captain that he was trying to run away from God. 'It's God who has sent this storm,' he said. 'Throw me overboard. Then the sea will be calm.'

As soon as Jonah had been thrown overboard, the sea grew calm. Jonah thought he would drown, but God sent a huge fish that swallowed him alive. Jonah was alone in the dark, inside the fish, for three days. He thought about how he had disobeyed God, and he was sorry. He told God so. After three days, the fish threw Jonah up on to a beach. Jonah had never been so glad to see daylight.

This time, Jonah went straight to Nineveh to tell the people God's message: 'In 40 days Nineveh will be destroyed!'

The people believed Jonah and were sorry for what they had done. Every one of them changed their ways. God was glad and (as Jonah had predicted) did not destroy them.

Jonah sat down outside the city, feeling angry and miserable. He grumbled to God. 'I knew you'd do this,' he said to God. 'That was why I tried to run away. I knew how kind you are. So now, just let me die!' But God didn't let Jonah die. Instead he made a plant grow up to shade him from the burning sun. Jonah felt better. But next day the plant withered up and the sun beat down on him. 'I was glad of that plant,' Jonah said. 'I'm sorry it's gone.'

God said to him, 'You're sorry for the plant, even though you did nothing to make it grow. But I gave life to all those people in Nineveh, and I take care of them, so don't you think I have a right to be sorry for them and forgive them?'

Jonah began to understand.

DISPLAYS FOR THE CHURCH

Box scenes

 Time duration: 30 minutes

You will need: large heavy-duty cardboard boxes, emulsion paint and brush, collage items (sandpaper, foil, crêpe paper, card, coloured paper, small boxes and tubes, metallic paper and so on), paint (optional), glue, thread, paper to make labels.

Making scenery in boxes is always a popular activity and works well for children in small groups or even in pairs. To prepare the boxes, first tape them up so there are no loose flaps, then cut them open carefully (see diagram) so that one box forms the basis for two sets of scenery. Have as many boxes as you can think of scenes for (such as outer space, ocean, glacier, desert, forest, city, village, countryside, industrial landscape), as God is with us in each of these.

When you cut open the boxes, you may find that odd flaps of card fall out, but these are easy to glue back into place. Once the glue is dry, paint the boxes inside with at least two coats of ordinary white emulsion to give a good basis for the collage work.

Provide a selection of collage materials (and paint if desired) and ask the children to create whichever scene is required. Labels made from laminated paper are a nice touch when the boxes are ready to go on display. Perhaps they could read something like 'God is with us in the desert; God is with us in outer space; God is with us in…' and so on. Use these as a starting point to talk about how God is with us wherever we go.

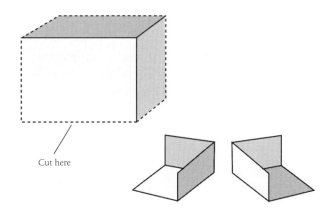

Cut here

SONGS FOR JONAH'S JOURNEY

- Wide, wide as the ocean (*Hymns Old and New* 559)
- God's love is deeper than the deepest ocean (*100 Hymns and Praise Songs for Kids*)

CRAFTS FOR JONAH'S JOURNEY

Lolly-stick photo frames

 Time duration: 10 minutes

You will need: lolly sticks (available from craft shops) painted in bright colours (eight per child), glue, digital camera and means of printing pictures.

You will need to have the consent of parents or carers to take the photographs for this activity. Before the session, practise taking and printing pictures to make sure you can print them out at the correct size for the frames and to see how much they will need to be trimmed. The printing for the pictures can be done at someone's home nearby if necessary.

As each child arrives, take a photograph of him or her with a digital camera. (You need to be quite sure that you have a photograph of everyone or there'll be tears!) While the pictures are being printed, the children can be getting on with another activity. When the photographs are ready, the children can make frames for their own photograph.

Lay the lolly sticks on top of the picture to form a frame, with two lolly sticks lying parallel on each side. Glue the sticks together where they overlap at the corners. You can then trim the picture and glue it to the back of the frame. Write a suitable message round the outside of the frame, such as 'God is with me'.

Junk modelling

 Time duration: 30 minutes

You will need: junk boxes, cartons and paper, glue (PVA, glue dots, glue gun, glue sticks), double-sided sticky tape, paint and brushes.

Invite the children to use the 'junk' and glue to make models of means of transport—cars, buses, trains, spaceships, boats, or anything they like. They can paint the models either at home or at a subsequent session or, if you have really fast-drying glue, later during the same session.

If the glossy finish on some cartons means that poster paint won't stick, you could try acrylic paint instead, or mix some flour in with the paint.

'Aeronautical engineering'

> ⏰ **Time duration:** 10 minutes
>
> **You will need:** sheets of A4 paper.

Making and testing paper aeroplanes is great fun and ideal for a church situation if it is raining, as naves usually give a nice long flight path! Try testing different designs to see which flies the best. If you can't remember how to fold a standard paper plane, there's a diagram below.

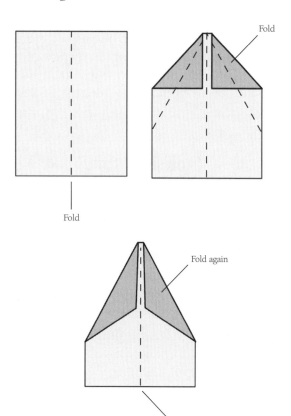

Fold

Fold

Fold again

Turn outside along this fold

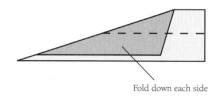

Fold down each side

Air race

Use the paper planes the children have made to conduct a mini competition to see which plane is most successful in a number of categories, such as longest time airborne, longest distance travelled, most spectacular aerobatic manoeuvre, highest flight, best low-level glide, and so on.

Fishy prayers

Using fish shapes for prayers is appropriate not only to remind everyone of what happened to Jonah, but also as a potent early Christian symbol. Have some fish shapes, cut from brightly coloured paper, ready to hand for each child. Spread out some netting (from a garden centre, or real fishing net if you have it). You might like to decorate the netting with strands of fabric or tissue paper to look like seaweed. Invite each child to write or draw their prayer on their fish shape and then attach it to the net. Someone standing ready with pieces of sticky tape could help with this. Leave the net on display as a reminder of the children's prayers.

Response prayers

You might want to try some prayers requiring a simple response, such as 'Guide us through life's storms' or 'Help us when times are rough'.

Session 4

PAUL'S JOURNEY

STORIES FOR PAUL'S JOURNEY

You will probably need to talk broadly about who Paul was and why he is famous. There are a number of stories about him that will catch the children's imagination, such as the story of his conversion on the road to Damascus, the story of Paul's and Silas' release from prison and the conversion of the guard, the story of the shipwreck and the viper on the island of Malta. If you are able to, memorise the stories and just tell them to the children. This is quite dramatic and should keep them in their seats.

Paul's journey took him to many different places around the eastern area of the Mediterranean Sea. A map of each of Paul's missionary journeys will help you to explain the routes he took. You could either use one large map for the whole group or organise it as a 'dot-to-dot' activity, with each person having his or her own map (or perhaps one between two). The story of Paul's journey to Malta is expanded in the synopsis below and in the holiday club programme, but you may choose to concentrate on a different incident from Paul's travels.

Story synopsis

Paul travelled all round the eastern part of the Mediterranean, telling people about Jesus and founding churches in many different places. A large portion of the New Testament is made up of letters he wrote to Christians in these places. The letters are known in the Bible either by the name of a single person he was writing to (such as Timothy or Philemon) or by a group name based on the place where they lived (such as the Ephesians, who were the people of Ephesus).

Paul's first missionary journey reached Cyprus and modern-day Turkey. With Barnabas and John Mark, he started at Antioch in Syria, from where they went to the coastal town of Seleucia. From there, they crossed the sea to Salamis on the island of Cyprus, then to Paphos on the other side of the island. Then they crossed the sea again and sailed to Perga, travelling to Antioch in Pisidia and then on to Iconium, Lystra, and Derbe. They then retraced their steps back to Lystra, Iconium and Antioch in Pisidia, went on to Perga and Attalia and then sailed back to Antioch in Syria.

Paul's second missionary journey reached as far as Greece. Again he started in Antioch in Syria, this time travelling with Silas. He travelled back to Derbe and Lystra, where he met Timothy. The three then travelled to Iconium and Antioch in Pisidia, and then to the Asia Minor port of Troas. From Troas they sailed to Neapolis in Macedonia and then travelled to Philippi, Thessalonica and Berea. Paul then travelled alone to Athens and Corinth, where he met Aquila and his wife Priscilla. The three sailed over the sea to Ephesus. Paul then sailed alone to Caesarea and travelled to Jerusalem before returning to Antioch in Syria.

Paul's third missionary journey started again in Antioch in Syria. He started as before by going via Tarsus to Derbe, Lystra and Antioch in Pisidia. He then travelled to Ephesus, round the coast, past Athens, back to Corinth, up to Thessalonica, then to Philippi and back by sea to Tyre, down to Caesarea and then Jerusalem.

Paul's final journey started in Caesarea. Paul journeyed to Tyre, and then he went by sea to Crete, then Malta, up to Syracuse in Sicily and on by sea to Rome, where he was held under house arrest and eventually put to death by the Romans.

There are lots of stories about Paul's adventures, one of which happened on Paul's final journey to Rome. Paul had been arrested by the authorities and it had been decided that he should be taken to Rome to be put on trial. The ship that was carrying Paul came into a very heavy storm. The sailors were frightened that they would die. They took down the sails and threw everything they didn't need overboard to try to stop the boat from sinking. Paul calmed everyone down and told them that no one would die. Eventually the ship came near to the island of Malta. Everyone from the ship managed to get to shore, but it was raining and very cold. Paul had gone to gather sticks so that they could light a fire, and was attacked by a viper—a particularly poisonous snake whose bite was known to be fatal. But Paul was unhurt and shook off the snake. There was not even a mark on his hand. The people were all amazed and local people on the island started bringing those who were unwell to him so that he could heal them.

DISPLAYS FOR THE CHURCH

Plotting Paul's journeys

 Time duration: 15 minutes

You will need: a large copy of a Bible map of the eastern Mediterranean with biblical names marked on it (see template on page 55), coloured self-adhesive dots.

Tell the children about Paul's journeys, using the summary of his travels below. Ask them to find the places he went to and mark them with the coloured dots on the map to show the journeys. Use different coloured dots for each journey.

Paul travelled all round the eastern part of the Mediterranean, telling people about Jesus and founding churches in many different places. A large portion of the New Testament is made up of letters he wrote to Christians in these places. The letters are known in the Bible either by the name of a single person he was writing to (such as Timothy or Philemon) or by a group name based on the place where they lived (such as the Ephesians, who were the people of Ephesus).

Travelling took a long time in those days because there were no cars or trains or planes. People walked, or rode a horse or donkey, or went by boat, so getting anywhere took a long time.

I've got a map here and we're going to work out where Paul travelled.

His first journey started at Antioch in Syria.

Paul crossed the sea to Salamis on the island of Cyprus, then to Paphos on the other side of the island. Then he crossed the sea again and travelled to Antioch in Pisidia, then on to Lystra, and Derbe, then back to Lystra, and Antioch in Pisidia, and on to Attalia. Then he sailed back to Antioch in Syria.

The second journey started in Antioch in Syria. Paul travelled to Tarsus, Derbe, Lystra, Antioch in Pisidia, Philippi, Thessalonica, Athens, Corinth, over the sea to Ephesus, by sea again to Caesarea, then to Jerusalem and back to Antioch in Syria.

The third journey started again in Antioch in Syria. Paul started as before by going to Tarsus, Derbe, Lystra and Antioch in Pisidia. Then he travelled to Ephesus, round the coast, past Athens, back to Corinth, up to Thessalonica, then to Philippi and back by sea to Tyre, down to Caesarea and then Jerusalem.

The final journey started in Caesarea. Paul journeyed to Tyre and then he went by sea to Crete, then Malta, up to Syracuse in Sicily and on by sea to Rome, where he was held prisoner under house arrest and eventually put to death by the Romans.

SONGS FOR PAUL'S JOURNEY

- O when the saints go marching in (*Junior Praise* 195)
- I, the Lord of sea and sky (*Hymns Old and New* 235)
- Seek ye first the kingdom of God (*Hymns Old and New* 442)

CRAFTS FOR PAUL'S JOURNEY

Jointed snakes

 Time duration: 15 minutes

You will need: thin coloured card, 30/60° set square, split-pin paper fasteners, hole punch, googly eyes, thin red ribbon, metallic pens, glue sticks, scissors.

Cut a series of identical diamond shapes from some thin card using a ruler and set square. Punch holes near the two wider angles. Get the children to decorate each segment of their snake with metallic pens. The two points of each segment can then be glued together to form a tube. Use split-pin paper fasteners to attach them together to make a snake that twists and turns. Use the thin red ribbon to make a flickering tongue, stick googly eyes on to the head end and shape the tail to a point.

FROM *FUN TO MAKE*, GILLIAN SOUTER (OFF THE SHELF PUBLISHING, 2001)

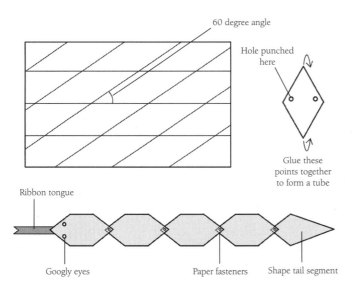

60 degree angle

Hole punched here

Glue these points together to form a tube

Ribbon tongue

Googly eyes   Paper fasteners   Shape tail segment

Paper chains

 Time duration: 10 minutes

You will need: strips of coloured paper, glue, stapler (optional).

Make paper chains in the usual way with strips of paper and glue or a stapler (for fast, strong joins). You could fasten everyone's short chains together to make a long one, to decorate your church. This activity will fit well with the story of Paul's imprisonment.

Prison pictures

 Time duration: 15 minutes

You will need: sheets of A4 paper, paint and brushes, black card, scissors, glue sticks or dots.

Give each child a piece of paper and ask them to paint a picture of 'freedom': how freedom would feel, what it might look like or a place where the children might feel free. Then have some black card ready cut to form a frame for the picture and bars across it. Mount the freedom picture behind the bars.

Postcards

 Time duration: 10 minutes

You will need: plain blank postcards, pens, crayons or pencils.

Get the children to design and write a postcard. They could either leave them in church on display or take them away and send them. If you wished, they could draw a picture of something they have learned in church that day and, in the writing, tell a friend about it. Alternatively, they could imagine the sort of postcards that Paul might have sent from one of his journeys or from prison.

Passports

 Time duration: 15 minutes

You will need: thick A5 paper folded to make booklets, photograph from digital camera (another print from the activity on page 23 or a fresh picture), pens, pencils, stamps and inkpads, a real passport.

Show the children a passport and explain what it is for. Show them the photograph and description and the stamps showing where the passport holder has travelled into and out of various countries.

Give each child two or three sheets of folded A5 paper and invite them to make their own passports. You will need a digital photograph of each child, which could be taken and printed out at the beginning of the session (with parental permission for the taking of the picture). Stick the photographs in the 'passports' and ask each child to add their names and other details. They can then decorate the pages using the stamps and inkpads.

GAMES FOR PAUL'S JOURNEY

Snakes and ladders

 Time duration: 20 minutes

You will need: snakes and ladders boards (one per group of four children), counters (one per child), dice (one per board).

To tie in with the story of the viper on Malta, play a game of snakes and ladders. Split the children into groups of four and give each group a board and a dice. Give each child a counter.

Get the children all to start their games at the same time, so that you have an overall winner as well as a winner in each group. Sweet vipers would make suitable prizes for the winners, but check food allergies before giving the sweets.

If you wanted to develop this idea into an extended activity for older children, they might enjoy the challenge of creating their own snakes and ladders game, which could be played later in the session by younger children or peers.

DISCUSSION ACTIVITIES FOR PAUL'S JOURNEY

Travelling in biblical times

 Time duration: 15–20 minutes

You will need: sheets of A4 paper, pens and/or pencils.

If you have plotted Paul's journeys on a large map, this will make a good starting point for a discussion about the difficulties involved in making journeys in those days and what an achievement it was for Paul to have travelled so widely.

Talk about how Paul wrote lots of letters to the places he had visited, where he had founded churches. Find these places on the map. Suggest that the children write letters to the PCC (or your church's governing body). If the children are not old enough to write a letter, just a sentence or a drawing will be fine. They

might write something about the Bible or about what they have learned in these sessions. If you do this, though, please make sure that a response is sent back to the children.

PRAYERS FOR PAUL'S JOURNEY

Paper chain prayers

If you have made paper chains with the children earlier in the session, you could use (and destroy) them for the prayers. Make sure the paper chains have been made using glue or sticky tape, rather than staples. Invite the children to stand close together in a group. Wrap the lengths of paper chain around the group. Say a brief prayer, perhaps thanking God that he forgives us when we do wrong. On the 'Amen', ask the children to break the paper chain, to symbolise the freedom Jesus has given us.

Map prayers

Use the map of Paul's journeys to thank God for Paul and others who ensured that the stories about Jesus spread beyond the Holy Land, to our own country and beyond. Pray for the people in the places on the map and in other places, too, where Christians might need our prayers.

Session 5

OUR CHRISTIAN JOURNEY

STORIES FOR OUR CHRISTIAN JOURNEY

After all the stories about biblical characters in the previous sessions, a passage about the Christian life from one of Paul's letters is an appropriate way to end the series. There are many to choose from, but Ephesians 3:14–21 would set the scene well and provide a positive conclusion to the programme.

I kneel in prayer to the Father. All beings in heaven and on earth receive their life from him. God is wonderful and glorious. I pray that his Spirit will make you become strong followers and that Christ will live in your hearts because of your faith. Stand firm and be deeply rooted in his love. I pray that you and all of God's people will understand what is called wide or long or high or deep. I want you to know all about Christ's love, although it is too wonderful to be measured. Then your lives will be filled with all that God is. I pray that Christ Jesus and the church will for ever bring praise to God. His power at work in us can do far more than we dare ask or imagine. Amen.

EPHESIANS 3:14–21

DISPLAYS FOR THE CHURCH

Christian journey collage

 Time duration: 25 minutes

You will need: a prepared collage board, collage items (paper, card, foam, magazine pictures, foil, fabric, leather, feathers, shiny materials and so on), glue.

Prepare a board for your collage. Get the children to decide what items they will need for the Christian journey. To help them in their thinking, start by asking how we know we're going in the right direction if we are on a journey to school, the shops or the swimming pool. Lead on from this to talk about how we find the way God wants us to go on our Christian journey. We will need a Bible for a map, prayer to ask for directions, fellowship with other Christians for companionship and mutual support, Jesus the light of the world as a torch, Jesus the bread of life for food, the water of baptism to keep us clean, and so on.

Spend some time working out how these things will be depicted. You may need labels to make clear exactly what the display is about. You could use pictures the children have made for each item, a collage made from magazine pictures or a mixture of the two. When the children have completed their work, read Ephesians 3:14–21 as a reflection on what they have done.

Footprints painting

 Time duration: 25 minutes

You will need: lining wallpaper, poster paint, brushes, bowls, water, soap, towels to wash feet, polythene dustsheets.

A footprint painting can be displayed in church as a frieze with a suitable caption or used as a background for the Christian journey collage above. Spread the lining paper on the floor, with polythene dustsheets underneath to protect the floor. Paint the soles of each child's feet (be prepared for laughter from the ticklish) and get them to walk down the length of the paper. Use lots of different colours to create an interesting effect.

SONGS FOR OUR CHRISTIAN JOURNEY

- One more step along the world I go (*Hymns Old and New* 405)
- The Spirit lives to set us free (*Hymns Old and New* 494)
- Will you come and follow me? (*Hymns Old and New* 560)
- Spirit of the living God (*Hymns Old and New* 454)
- The Lord's my shepherd (*Hymns Old and New* 490)

Footprints Bible verses

 Time duration: 15 minutes

You will need: sheets of A4 paper, poster paint, brushes, foot-washing equipment as above, foot-shaped print blocks (optional).

Give each child a sheet of paper and either get them to do prints of their own feet or give them small foot-shaped print blocks to create a picture. The print blocks are made by cutting foot shapes from some craft foam, gluing them to corrugated card and trimming round the edge. Add handles to the block and then apply paint (sparingly).

Have spare sheets of paper to hand, so the children can get the hang of the technique before doing their pictures. Add a Bible verse, choosing either a verse from Ephesians 3:14–21 (such as 'Stand firm and be deeply rooted in Christ's love') or ask the children to add a Bible verse of their choice (perhaps a memory verse or a verse from a well-known song).

COOKING FOR OUR CHRISTIAN JOURNEY

Food for the journey

 Time duration: 20 minutes

You will need: sliced bread, butter or spread, a selection of sandwich fillings.

This would be a good way to round off the holiday club as a final activity, but make sure you have plenty of time for it. Talk about what food you might take with you.

Invite the children to help you make some sandwiches and then go for a short walk to a place where there is some grass for the children to sit on. Enjoy the picnic: take some juice and biscuits, too. Picnic inside if it is raining.

Bread rolls

If time and facilities allow, you may wish to consider making your own bread rolls (see recipe on page 46). When baked and cooled, these can then be filled with the sandwich filling provided.

Biscuits

If time and facilities allow, the children might like to make their own biscuits to take on the picnic (see recipe on page 46).

Christian journey goodie bags

 Time duration: 10–15 minutes

You will need: plain white A5 or A4 envelopes, colouring pens, stickers and/or coloured paper and glue to decorate the bags, items with which to fill the bags (see suggestions below).

Cut off the envelope flap or seal it inside the envelope, then cut out an elliptical hole towards the top of each envelope, leaving at least 2cm of paper above the hole to give the handle some strength. Invite each child to write their name on their bag and decorate it as they choose.

The bag can then be filled with symbols from each of the holiday club sessions. If children haven't taken home everything they made at the club, you could use these items. Alternatively (and perhaps more probably, as children are usually keen to take the fruits of their labours home to share with friends and family), you could add your own symbols, such as a feather to represent Noah's dove; a small stone (a pretty polished one would be attractive) for Moses' desert; a paper plane as a reminder of Jonah's attempted escape from God; a few links of chain to represent Paul's imprisonment; and a small printed footprint, perhaps with a Bible verse inscribed on it, as a reminder of our own journey. There is no reason not to include a small packet of sweets to represent the fact that we need sustenance on our journey.

GAMES FOR OUR CHRISTIAN JOURNEY

As this is the final workshop in the series, some party games would be appropriate. Use games you know the children enjoy, or you might include some of the ideas below.

Guess the place

 Time duration: 10 minutes

You will need: pieces of card with place names written on them.

Tailor the places you use to the ages of the children who will be playing. If the children are young, use the names of places in your locality. You might even make it as simple as 'school', 'shop', 'swings', and so on. Use local towns for slightly older children and different countries for the oldest ones.

To play the game, give a child one of the location cards, but instruct them not to show it to anyone else. The others have to guess where that place is by asking questions, to which the child with the card can answer only 'yes' or 'no'. Put a limit on the number of questions asked. If the location is not guessed within this limit, put the card to the back of the pile and choose another location and another child.

Modes of transport

 Time duration: 10 minutes

You will need: pieces of card with modes of transport written on them (one set per group).

Put the children into three or four groups, with an equal number of children in each group. Set the groups apart from each other. Sit in the middle of the room. Get one child from each group to come up to you to collect a card, return to their group and mime the mode of transport on the card to the rest of the group. Once the group has guessed the mime, the next person in the group goes up for a card and so on, until all the cards for that group have been used up. The winning group is the one that guesses all the

modes of transport first. Ideas might include flying, walking, driving, sailing, cycling, horse riding, motor biking, using a submarine, and so on.

Guess who?

 Time duration: 10 minutes

You will need: items of clothing or objects to provide hints.

Recap the holiday club by testing the children on the people they have learned about in the past week. Get a grown-up helper to dress up or bring an object associated with one of the biblical characters from the previous four workshops, and see if the children know who is being represented.

Directions game

Put the children in pairs. Tell one child in each pair that they need to conduct their partner to a place, but they mustn't tell the partner where the place is. Instead they must give them directions on how to get there: for example, 'turn to your right and take ten paces' and so on. Once the partner has reached the destination, let the children swap roles and give them another destination.

DISCUSSION ACTIVITIES FOR OUR CHRISTIAN JOURNEY

Where are we going on holiday?

 Time duration: 10 minutes

You will need: a map of the world or the country where you live, self-adhesive coloured dots.

Have a map of the world on which to mark places where the children are going on holiday. Talk about what the children know about these places and how people might live in these countries. If you are unlikely to have many children going on holidays abroad, have a map of your own country. Use the activity as a starter for prayers about the places we will be visiting on holiday, and lead this in to prayers for the time when you will all be coming together again after the holidays.

PRAYERS FOR OUR CHRISTIAN JOURNEY

Praying for others

Use the above activity as a starting point for prayers. Pray for people who live in the places we will visit and for all travellers to and from those places. Pray for the places that we don't want to visit on holiday because of drought, famine, war or oppression.

Balloon release prayers

Arrange in advance for some balloons to be filled with helium. During the session, ask the children for ideas about what we might pray to God for or about to help with our life journey. Gather the children outside for the prayer. Remind the children that we don't know what turns our lives may take, any more than we know where the balloons will end up when we let go of them. Say a short prayer using the ideas the children have contributed about our life journey. Give each child a balloon or two. On the 'Amen' of the prayer, everyone should release their balloon and watch it float away.

If you wish to attach written prayers to the balloons, you could do this, but be careful that personal information is not included.

Door prayers

If your sessions have taken place in church, why not say a final prayer gathered round the church door as preparation for leaving the holiday club and resuming our Christian journeys. If your venue was a church hall or other meeting place, a final prayer could be said in the same way, for the children to think about their Christian journey as they leave the room. Say the prayer while the children are still gathered as a group and before they are collected by their parents and carers.

Appendix 1

The following sheets can either be photocopied or, alternatively, downloaded from the website: www.barnabasinchurches.org.uk/pdfs/biblejourneys.pdf.

- Registration form
- Parental consent form
- Signing in and out form

REGISTRATION FORM

Child's details	
Name:	Date of birth: / /
Address:	
Telephone:	
Details of any allergies:	
Other medical conditions/anything else we should be aware of:	
Name of doctor:	
Surgery:	Telephone:
Emergency contact details:	
Home telephone number:	
Emergency telephone/mobile number:	
Any other relevant emergency contact details:	

 Reproduced with permission from *Bible Journeys Holiday Club* published by BRF 2011 (978 1 84101 808 9) www.barnabasinchurches.org.uk

PARENTAL CONSENT FORM

In the event of an emergency, we need your consent to administer First Aid to your child and, if necessary, take them to hospital for medical treatment. We have trained First Aiders among our helpers or can call on local First Aiders.

Occasionally, photographs of the children may be taken during workshops for one of the following purposes: (i) for our records; (ii) for children to use during workshops; (iii) for reporters from the local newspaper who sometimes visit to report on the workshops; (iv) for training for your helpers.

As we have no toilet facilities in the church building, children needing to use the toilet are accompanied to .... to use the toilet there. We also sometimes arrange for activities to take place in the churchyard, and we may want to take the children (properly supervised, with a ratio of two adults to every six children for younger children, and two adults to every eight children for older children) on a short walk in the nearby vicinity. We will notify you in advance if outside activities are planned.

I consent/do not consent to the above in respect of:

- First Aid
- Photographs for club records
- Photographs for workshop activities
- Photographs for the local press
- Supervised activity outside the church building

Delete as appropriate

Form completed by: _____

Relationship to child: _____

Signature: _____

Date: ____ / ____ / _____

SIGNING IN AND OUT FORM

Session type: _____

Date: _____

CHILD'S NAME	TO BE COLLECTED BY	SIGNED IN	SIGNED OUT	NOTES

 Reproduced with permission from *Bible Journeys Holiday Club* published by BRF 2011 (978 1 84101 808 9) www.barnabasinchurches.org.uk

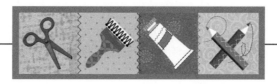

Appendix 2

The following session plans can either be photocopied or, alternatively, downloaded from the website: www.barnabasinchurches.org.uk/pdfs/biblejourneys.pdf.

- Session plan for Noah's journey
- Session plan for Moses' journey
- Session plan for Jonah's journey
- Session plan for Paul's journey
- Session plan for our Christian journey
- Blank session plan

SESSION PLAN FOR NOAH'S JOURNEY

Activities can be removed, added or altered according to the ability and circumstances of your group. Provide extension activities for children who finish early. For example, the children could use watercolours to produce pictures of Noah's experiences, or make bubble prints by blowing (and only blowing) down a straw into a mixture of watered-down paint and washing-up liquid to create coloured bubbles, then laying paper over them.

THE STORY OF NOAH

GENESIS 6:1—9:17

Suitable for children aged 5–11

Time	Activity	Details
10 minutes	Registration	Pen, paper, registration forms, badges and blanks
10 minutes	Story	The story of Noah
15 minutes	Craft (3 rotating groups)	Cork boats
15 minutes	Craft (3 rotating groups)	Rainbow mobiles
15 minutes	Craft (3 rotating groups)	Chalk pavement art
10 minutes	Break	Refreshments
15 minutes	Craft (3 rotating groups)	Cardboard tube animals (to display against ark backdrop)
15 minutes	Craft (3 rotating groups)	Animal masks
15 minutes	Craft (3 rotating groups)	Rainbow doves
30 minutes	Worship with parents and carers	Rise and shine Have you heard the raindrops? Who put the colours in the rainbow? Prayers for Noah's journey

 Reproduced with permission from *Bible Journeys Holiday Club* published by BRF 2011 (978 1 84101 808 9) www.barnabasinchurches.org.uk

SESSION PLAN FOR MOSES' JOURNEY

Activities can be removed, added or altered according to the ability and circumstances of your group. Provide extension activities for children who finish early. For example, encourage the children to make sandy pictures using card or stiff paper, coloured sand or gravel (available from aquatic suppliers) and glue, with string to mark boundaries between different colours; or ask them to draw what they think the promised land might look like.

EXODUS; TEN COMMANDMENTS; REACHING THE PROMISED LAND

EXODUS 12:31–42; 14:5–31; EXODUS 20:1–17; DEUTERONOMY 34:1–7; JOSHUA 3:1–17

Suitable for children aged 5–11

Time	Activity	Details
10 minutes	Registration	Pen, paper, registration forms, badges and blanks
10 minutes	Story	Escape from Egypt
10 minutes	Song	One more step along the world I go
10 minutes	Craft	Compasses
10 minutes	Craft	Packed suitcases
10 minutes	Game	Memory game
10 minutes	Break	Refreshments
10 minutes	Story	The Ten Commandments
15 minutes	Craft	Personal arks
15 minutes	Display for the church	Road signs
10 minutes	Story	Reaching the promised land
30 minutes	Worship with parents and carers	One more step along the world I go How did Moses cross the Red Sea? Will you come and follow me? Prayers for Moses' journey

SESSION PLAN FOR JONAH'S JOURNEY

Activities can be removed, added or altered according to the ability and circumstances of your group. Provide extension activities for children who finish early. For example, provide collage materials for the children to create a fishy scene, such as a selection of foils, coloured cellophane, tissue and crêpe paper.

THE STORY OF JONAH

JONAH 1:1—4:11

Suitable for children aged 5–11

Time	Activity	Details
10 minutes	Registration	Pen, paper, registration forms, badges and blanks
10 minutes	Story	The story of Jonah
30 minutes	Craft	Junk modelling
10 minutes	Break	Refreshments
30 minutes	Display for the church	Box scenes
10 minutes	Craft and game (3 rotating groups)	'Aeronautical engineering'
10 minutes	Song (3 rotating groups)	Wide, wide as the ocean
10 minutes	Craft (3 rotating groups)	Lolly-stick photo frames
30 minutes	Worship with parents and carers	Wide, wide as the ocean God's love is deeper than the deepest ocean Prayers for Jonah's journey

 Reproduced with permission from *Bible Journeys Holiday Club* published by BRF 2011 (978 1 84101 808 9) www.barnabasinchurches.org.uk

SESSION PLAN FOR PAUL'S JOURNEY

Activities can be removed, added or altered according to the ability and circumstances of your group. Provide extension activities for children who finish early, such as snakes and ladders, or discussion on travelling in biblical times.

ROAD TO DAMASCUS; PAUL IN PRISON; SHIPWRECK; ON THE ISLAND OF MALTA

ACTS 9:1–19; 16:16–40; 27:1–44; ACTS 28:1–10

Suitable for children aged 5–11

Time	Activity	Details
10 minutes	Registration	Pen, paper, registration forms, badges and blanks
5 minutes	Story	The road to Damascus
15 minutes	Display for the church	Plotting Paul's journeys
15 minutes	Craft	Passports
5 minutes	Story	Paul and Silas in prison
10 minutes	Craft	Paper chains
15 minutes	Craft	Prison pictures
10 minutes	Break	Refreshments
15 minutes	Craft	Postcards
5 minutes	Story	The shipwreck
5 minutes	Story	On the island of Malta
15 minutes	Craft	Jointed snakes
30 minutes	Worship with parents and carers	O when the saints go marching in I, the Lord of sea and sky Seek ye first the kingdom of God Prayers for Paul's journey

SESSION PLAN FOR OUR CHRISTIAN JOURNEY

Activities can be removed, added or altered according to the ability and circumstances of your group. Provide extension activities for children who finish early, such as footprints Bible verse cards or the 'Guess who?' game.

CHRIST'S LOVE FOR US

EPHESIANS 3:14–21

Suitable for children aged 5–11

Time	Activity	Details
10 minutes	Registration	Pen, paper, registration forms, badges and blanks
10 minutes	Discussion activities	Where are we going on holiday?
25 minutes	Display for the church	Christian journey collage or Footprints painting
20 minutes	Cooking	Food for the journey
15 minutes	Break	Refreshments (picnic)
10 minutes	Game	Guess the place
10 minutes	Game	Modes of transport
10 minutes	Game	Directions game
10 minutes	Prayers	'Where are we going on holiday?' prayers
30 minutes	Worship with parents and carers	One more step along the world I go The Spirit lives to set us free Will you come and follow me? Spirit of the living God The Lord's my shepherd

 Reproduced with permission from *Bible Journeys Holiday Club* published by BRF 2011 (978 1 84101 808 9) www.barnabasinchurches.org.uk

BLANK SESSION PLAN

STORY _____

BIBLE REFERENCE _____

Age range _____

Time	Activity	Details

Appendix 3

BASIC RECIPES

PLAY DOUGH

You will need:

- 200g plain flour
- 225g salt
- 2 tsp cream of tartar
- 2 tbsp cooking oil
- 325ml boiling water
- Food dye if desired

Mix the flour, salt, cream of tartar and cooking oil together in a bowl. Add two cups of boiling water (just boiled, straight from the kettle). If you want the dough coloured, adding food dye to the water will help the even distribution of colour through the mix. Knead with a hand-held mixer or machine (the dough will be too hot for your hands). Allow the dough to cool (but don't let it crust over) before packing it away in a plastic bag.

BREAD DOUGH

You will need:

- 400g strong plain flour
- 2 level tsp sugar
- 2 level tsp dried yeast (the fast-action variety)
- 1.5 level tsp salt
- 250ml warm water
- 2 tbsp olive oil
- 2 mixing bowls
- Mixing spoon
- Sieve
- Clean tea towel
- Greaseproof paper
- Baking tray
- Cooling rack

Sift the flour, sugar, yeast and salt into a bowl. (If you are using yeast that needs to be reconstituted in water first, follow the instructions on the packet.) Add the water and oil and knead well. Cover with a clean tea towel and leave in a warm place for approximately one hour until it has doubled in size.

Turn the dough out on to a floured surface and knead again evenly until smooth. Divide the dough and shape as required. Place finished products on a greased and floured baking tray. Cover with the tea towel and leave until doubled in size.

Bake in the centre of a preheated oven at Gas Mark 5 or 190°C for 45–50 minutes for a loaf and 15–20 minutes for rolls, until they are golden brown and the base sounds hollow when tapped. Cool on a wire rack.

BISCUIT MIX

You will need:

- 300g plain flour (plus extra for flouring surfaces)
- A pinch of salt
- 1 tsp baking powder
- 1 tsp nutmeg and/or 1 tsp ground ginger (if making ginger biscuits)
- 100g butter or margarine
- 100g soft brown sugar
- 2 eggs
- 60g golden syrup
- Mixing bowl and spoon or hand-held mixer
- Baking parchment or greaseproof paper
- Rolling pins
- Biscuit cutters
- Pencils
- Hand-washing facilities

Put the flour, salt, baking powder and spice into a bowl. Rub in the butter or margarine and then stir in the sugar. Beat the eggs with the golden syrup and add to the mixture. Mix well either by hand or with a hand-held mixer.

Divide the dough into pieces sufficient for each child. Have a surface ready for rolling: pieces of well-floured baking parchment or greaseproof paper on your normal table covering work well and are disposable later. The dough should be rolled out to about 5mm thickness and then the biscuits can be cut out.

Get the children to place their biscuits on a named piece of baking parchment. The biscuits will need to be baked in an oven preheated to Gas Mark 3 or 160°C for about 18 minutes, but keep an eye on them.

PEPPERMINT CREAMS

You will need:

- 1–2 tbsp milk
- A few drops peppermint oil
- 250–300g icing sugar (sifted)
- Mixing bowls
- Mixing spoons
- Rolling pin
- Small pastry cutters
- Baking tray
- Greaseproof paper
- Small cardboard gift boxes (optional)
- Ribbon (optional)

Put the milk in a bowl and add the peppermint oil. Gradually add the icing sugar until a stiff mixture is formed. Turn the mixture out on to greaseproof paper that has been dusted with sifted icing sugar, and roll out to 0.5cm in thickness. Cut into rounds with a small pastry cutter. Gather the trimmings, re-roll and re-cut until all the mixture is used up.

Place sweets on a baking tray lined with greaseproof paper until dry. If desired, have available some small attractive boxes to put the sweets into when they are dry. (Makes approximately 20 sweets.)

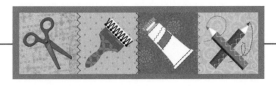

Appendix 4

BASIC CRAFT SKILLS

PREPARING A COLLAGE BOARD

You will need: sheet of MDF board, measuring approximately 600mm x 1000mm, lining wallpaper, masking tape and/or double-sided sticky tape.

Cover the boards with lining wallpaper. The children can then collage straight on to the boards and the finished work can be displayed in the church against a rail or pillar.

Having two collage boards will afford you extra flexibility, as you can keep the children's work on display for longer with one board on display and the other one in the course of preparation.

PREPARING A BANNER OR HANGING

You will need: a large rectangle of hessian or heavyweight upholstery or curtain fabric, measuring approximately 0.5 metre long by 1 metre wide or to suit the area where you wish to hang it, broom handle or length of dowel or pipe, thick twine or curtain cord, sewing thread and needle or a sewing machine.

Hem round all sides of the fabric. Turn a casing along one of the shorter sides through which the broom handle can be threaded. Attach the twine or curtain cord to the ends of the broom handle and hang the banner from an available hook. Alternatively, omit the casing and pole and hang the banner on a bare wall, using Blu-tack or masking tape to secure in place (although the heaviness of the fabric will determine whether or not this will be a satisfactory method of fixing it).

MAKING A FEELY BOX

You will need: small cardboard boxes (half case of wine size is ideal), off-cuts of fabric, elastic, scissors, sewing thread and needle, PVA glue.

Cut some fabric to make a sleeve to fit round the open end of the box. Make a casing along one end. Sew or glue the side seam of the fabric, making sure that the sleeve fits around the box and that you can still get to both ends of the casing.

When the glue is dry, thread the casing with elastic, pull it through and tie the ends together so that the elastic expands enough for you to get your hand inside easily, but is tight enough to make it hard to see what is inside. Fit the sleeve over the box and glue in place so that it comes well over the open end of the box.

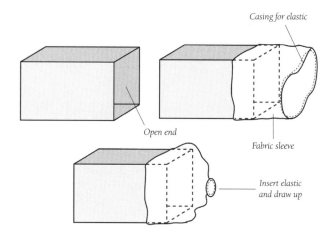

Casing for elastic

Open end

Fabric sleeve

Insert elastic and draw up

Given below are suggestions for small objects that might be placed inside the feely box for each of the five holiday club sessions.

Session 1: Noah's journey

- A ornamental dove
- A feather
- A small umbrella

Session 2: Moses' journey

- A folded map
- A small shoe
- Some small stones or gravel

Session 3: Jonah's journey

- A fish shape
- A model boat
- A plant cutting (chose something sturdy such as an evergreen, but avoid yew, which is poisonous)

Session 4: Paul's journey

- Small plastic or rubber toy snake
- Short length of chain
- A model boat

Session 5: Our Christian journey

- A 'sturdy' bread roll
- A bottle of water
- A cross
- You may wish to include something symbolic that you use for prayers, such as beads, a bell or a simple model of praying hands

Appendix 5

TEMPLATES

The following templates can be either photocopied or downloaded from the website:
www.barnabasinchurches.org.uk/pdfs/biblejourneys.pdf.

DOVE

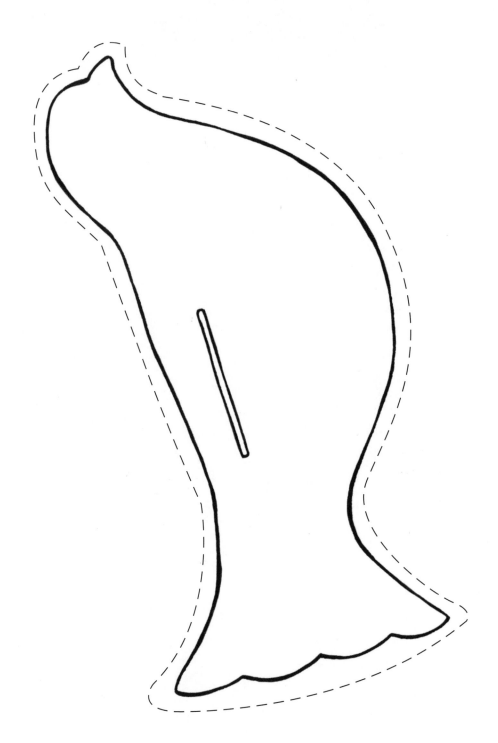

 Reproduced with permission from *Bible Journeys Holiday Club* published by BRF 2011 (978 1 84101 808 9) www.barnabasinchurches.org.uk

BIBLICAL MAP OF THE EASTERN MEDITERRANEAN REGION

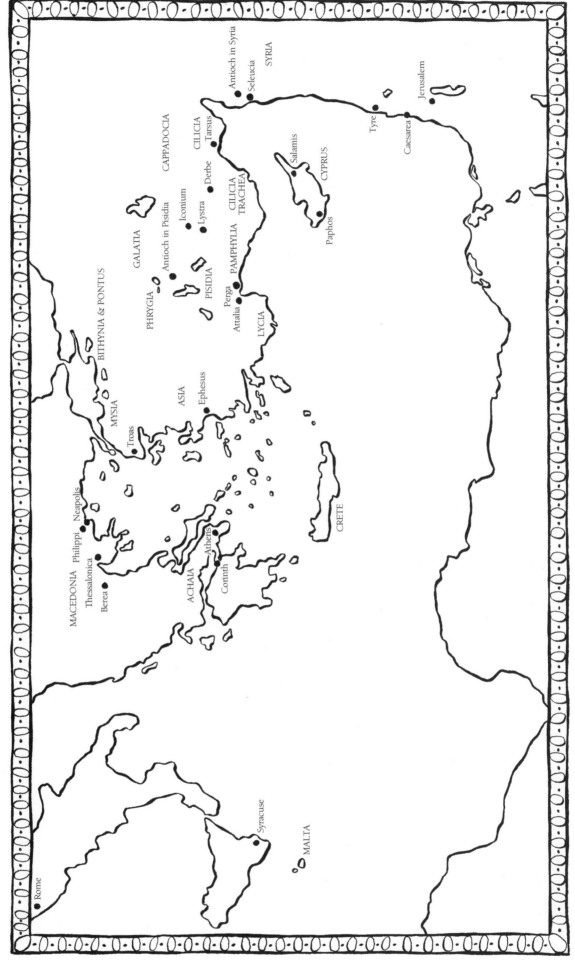

Antioch in Syria
Seleucia
SYRIA
Tarsus
CILICIA
CAPPADOCIA
Derbe
Iconium
Lystra
Antioch in Pisidia
GALATIA
PHRYGIA
PISIDIA
CILICIA TRACHEA
PAMPHYLIA
Perga
Attalia
LYCIA
Salamis
CYPRUS
Paphos
Tyre
Caesarea
Jerusalem
BITHYNIA & PONTUS
ASIA
Ephesus
MYSIA
Troas
Neapolis
Philippi
MACEDONIA
Thessalonica
Berea
ACHAIA
Athens
Corinth
CRETE
Syracuse
MALTA
Rome

BIBLIOGRAPHY

Listed below are the resources that have provided inspiration and ideas for this book. A wide selection of Bibles in different versions is very useful to find the right translation for a particular story (it won't always be a children's Bible). Alongside Christian material, general activity books and children's storybooks can often be adapted to illustrate the theme.

BIBLES AND BIBLE STORIES

The Barnabas Children's Bible (Barnabas, 2007)

The Dramatised Bible (Marshall Pickering, 1989)

The Lion Children's Bible (Lion, 1981)

International Children's Bible (Nelson Word, 1983)

Contemporary English Version of the Bible (HarperCollins, 2000)

New Revised Standard Version of the Bible (HarperCollins, 1989)

The Children's Illustrated Bible (Dorling Kindersley, 1994)

The Usborne Children's Bible (Usborne, 2000)

My Book of Bible Stories (Lion, 2002)

Stories Jesus Told, Nick Butterworth and Mick Inkpen (Marshall Pickering, 1996)

SONG BOOKS

Junior Praise (Marshall Pickering, 1986)

Hymns Old and New (Kevin Mayhew, 1996)

Kidsource (Kevin Mayhew, 2002)

CHRISTIAN RESOURCE BOOKS

Godly Play, Jerome W. Berryman (Augsburg, 1991)

Young Children and Worship, Sonya M. Stewart and Jerome W. Berryman (Westminster John Knox Press, 1989)

Following Jesus, Sonya M. Stewart and Jerome W. Berryman (Geneva Press, 2000)

Teaching Godly Play, Sonya M. Stewart and Jerome W. Berryman (Abingdon Press, 1995)

The Complete Guide to Godly Play, Volumes 1–5, Jerome W. Berryman (Living the Good News, 2002

Theme Games, Lesley Pinchbeck (Scripture Union, 1993)

Theme Games 2, Lesley Pinchbeck (Scripture Union, 2002)

The 'E' Book: Essential Prayers and Activities for Faith at Home, Gill Ambrose (National Society/Church House Publishing, 2000)

Children Aloud, Gordon and Ronni Lamont (National Society/Church House Publishing, 1997)

One Hundred and One Ideas for Creative Prayers, Judith Merrell (Scripture Union, 1995)

New Ideas for Creative Prayer, Judith Merrell (Scripture Union, 2001)

The Gospels Unplugged, Lucy Moore (Barnabas, 2002)

The Lord's Prayer Unplugged, Lucy Moore (Barnabas, 2004)

Here's One I Made Earlier, Kathryn Copsey (Scripture Union, 1995)

Here's Another One I Made Earlier, Christine Orme (Scripture Union, 2000)

Come and Join the Celebration, John Muir and Betty Pedley (National Society/Church House Publishing, 2001)

Welcome to the Lord's Table, Margaret Withers (Barnabas, 1999)

CHILDREN'S ACTIVITY BOOKS

Festive Fun, Gillian Souter (Off the Shelf Publishing, 2001)

Fun to Make, Gillian Souter (Off the Shelf Publishing, 2001)

Beads and Badges, Gillian Souter (Off the Shelf Publishing, 1999)

Cool Stuff, Susie Lacome (MQ Publications, 2002)

Fun to Make and Do, Hannah Tofts and Annie Owen (Two-Can Publishing, 1990)

What Shall I Do Today?, Ray Gibson (Usborne, 1995)

Make and Colour Paper Planes, Clare Beaton (b small publishing, 2000)

OTHER RESOURCES

How to Eat: The Pleasures and Principles of Good Food, Nigella Lawson (Chatto & Windus, 1998)

THROUGH THE YEAR WITH JESUS!

A once-a-month children's programme for small churches

As a sequel to *Not Sunday, Not School!*, Eleanor Zuercher has developed an exciting further year's worth of themed material—this time based on aspects of the life and teaching of Jesus.

Once again, the material is explored through a wealth of creative and interactive activities, with a pattern that enables children to feel involved, whatever their age or level of attendance. Each session is designed to last approximately two hours, although this can be shortened or lengthened according to need. The book is packed with fresh suggestions for Bible stories, practical ideas for creating a display for the church, and a host of brand new craft activities, games and ideas for creative prayer. The material also includes an exciting summer activity programme based on the 'I am' sayings of Jesus.

Through-the-year themes include:

- Baptism
- Faith
- Prayer
- Miracles
- Parables
- Blessings
- Forgiveness
- Transfiguration
- Jesus' friends
- Jesus and me
- God with us

ISBN 978 1 84101 578 1   £9.99
Available from your local Christian bookshop or, in case of difficulty, direct from BRF using the order form on page 63. You may also visit the website www.brfonline.org.uk.

CREATIVE IDEAS FOR ALL-AGE CHURCH

12 through-the-year programmes for informal church services and special one-off events

KAREN BULLEY

The twelve themes in this book contain a wealth of creative worship ideas, all designed to encourage the church family to listen to each other's stories. Through listening and worshipping together in a less formal setting, the material promotes creative thinking and enables people of all ages to learn together in worship and grow in faith as part of God's family.

Each theme includes introductory reflections on the season of the year; a biblical context; ideas for a visual display; age-specific activities; suggestions for sharing a meal; suggestions for reflections, prayers and sung worship and, finally, ideas for taking the theme further.

The themes can be used to plan stand-alone worship programmes or to follow the pattern of the Christian year, giving an ideal opportunity for a once-a-month exploration of the colour, creativity and individuality of each season. Some themes are based on Bible stories or issues relevant to the church family, while others use abstract ideas designed to promote lateral thinking.

The material offers a wide range of practical ideas and fun (or reflective) activities designed to give choice to those planning the worship. A pick-and-mix approach provides flexibility for the length and setting of worship.

Themes include:

* Gifts, skills and talents (Epiphany)
* Lent
* Unity (Holy Week)
* Celebrating life (Easter)
* Sharing our story (Ascension)
* Prayer (Pentecost)
* Summer outings
* Quiet spaces
* Harvest
* Sharing our concerns
* Advent
* Christmas

ISBN 978 1 84101 663 4   £7.99

Available from your local Christian bookshop or, in case of difficulty, direct from BRF using the order form on page 63. You may also visit the website www.brfonline.org.uk.

CREATIVE IDEAS FOR QUIET CORNERS

14 visual prayer ideas for quiet moments with children

LYNN CHAMBERS

One of the most significant responsibilities of any Christian parent, godparent, grandparent, minister or children's work leader is to help children learn what it means to speak and listen to God through prayer. Yet space for prayer is often, at best, pushed into a corner.

This book offers 14 creative suggestions designed to encourage both adults and children to find space for prayer, by creating a physical prayer space in the home or in a place of worship that can be visited and enjoyed. The materials could be used to form an ongoing sacred space throughout the months of the year or offered at particular times—for example, during a school holiday or a season of the year such as Christmas or Easter.

Each prayer idea uses simple, easily found materials and needs minimal space to create a quiet, reflective corner. All the materials for creating such a space have been carefully chosen to nurture an understanding for both adults and children of what it means to come into the presence of God, to listen and to be still. Alongside the visual tableaux, the book offers practical support to enable people of all ages and abilities to move at their own pace and at their own level into a sense of quietness and prayer.

Each quiet corner includes the following elements:

- Introduction
- Getting started
- Stilling
- Bible focus
- Staying with the story
- Living with the story
- Prayer response
- Living the journey

ISBN 978 1 84101 546 0   *£6.99*

Available from your local Christian bookshop or, in case of difficulty, direct from BRF using the order form on page 63. You may also visit the website www.brfonline.org.uk.

INSTANT GAMES FOR CHILDREN

101 fun-filled children's games

SUSAN L. LINGO

Play 101 new 'use-them-anywhere' games. It's as easy as 1… 2… 3.

Collect 14 inexpensive, everyday items such as two ping-pong balls, a bag of balloons and two skipping ropes—things that are readily available. Drop the items into a bag… and you're ready!

You'll always be prepared with a fun activity, child-pleasing party idea or action-packed game. They're in the bag, ready at a moment's notice.

Use the games to:

- Help children to get to know each other better
- Build friendships among classmates
- Let children burn off extra energy
- Encourage cooperation and teamwork
- Create a fun, welcoming atmosphere

All the games come complete with instructions, rules and quick and easy explanations, so you will have your children laughing and playing in no time at all.

ISBN 978 1 84101 591 0   £6.99

Available from your local Christian bookshop or, in case of difficulty, direct from BRF using the order form on page 63. You may also visit the website www.brfonline.org.uk.

THE ENCYCLOPEDIA OF BIBLE CRAFTS

187 fun-filled, easy-to-do craft activities for children

EDITED BY LAURIE CASTAÑEDA

Children love doing craft activities—and children's leaders love crafts that connect children to Bible truths! This bumper collection of creative, fun-filled and easy-to-do Bible crafts is designed to inspire and enthuse leaders and children alike as they explore the Bible together.

Each tried-and-tested craft is designed to fit into any Bible-based children's work programme, whether that's on a Sunday, midweek, or a one-off special event. Every single book of the Bible is covered, with crafts to illustrate many key Bible passages. The crafts are easy to prepare, easy to do and require very little equipment or materials.

Alongside the craft activities you will also find:

- An age guide for each craft
- A Bible reference
- A Bible point
- 'You will need' list
- Handy hints
- Step-by-step instructions
- Teaching point

Includes photocopy permission for all craft templates.

ISBN 978 1 84101 590 3   £12.99

Available from your local Christian bookshop or, in case of difficulty, direct from BRF using the order form on page 63. You may also visit the website www.brfonline.org.uk.

ORDERFORM

REF	TITLE	PRICE	QTY	TOTAL
578 1	Through the Year with Jesus	£9.99		
663 4	Creative Ideas for All-Age Church	£7.99		
546 0	Creative Ideas for Quiet Corners	£6.99		
591 0	Instant Games for Children	£6.99		
590 3	The Encyclopedia of Bible Crafts	£12.99		

Postage and packing	
Donation	
TOTAL	

POSTAGE AND PACKING CHARGES

Order value	UK	Europe	Surface	Air Mail
£7.00 & under	£1.25	£3.00	£3.50	£5.50
£7.10–£30.00	£2.25	£5.50	£6.50	£10.00
Over £30.00	FREE	prices on request		

Name _____ Account Number _____

Address _____

_____ Postcode _____

Telephone Number_____

Email _____

Payment by: ❑ Cheque ❑ Mastercard ❑ Visa ❑ Postal Order ❑ Maestro

Card no ⬜⬜⬜⬜ ⬜⬜⬜⬜ ⬜⬜⬜⬜ ⬜⬜⬜⬜ ▨▨▨

Valid from ⬜⬜⬜⬜ Expires ⬜⬜⬜⬜ Issue no. ▨▨▨

Security code* ⬜⬜⬜ *Last 3 digits on the reverse of the card. ESSENTIAL IN ORDER TO PROCESS YOUR ORDER   Shaded boxes for Maestro use only

Signature _____ Date _____

All orders must be accompanied by the appropriate payment.

Please send your completed order form to:
BRF, 15 The Chambers, Vineyard, Abingdon OX14 3FE
Tel. 01865 319700 / Fax. 01865 319701 Email: enquiries@brf.org.uk

❑ Please send me further information about BRF publications.

Available from your local Christian bookshop.   BRF is a Registered Charity

About
brf:

BRF is a registered charity and also a limited company, and has been in existence since 1922. Through all that we do—producing resources, providing training, working face-to-face with adults and children, and via the web—we work to resource individuals and church communities in their Christian discipleship through the Bible, prayer and worship.

Our Barnabas children's team works with primary schools and churches to help children under 11, and the adults who work with them, to explore Christianity creatively and to bring the Bible alive.

To find out more about BRF and its core activities and ministries, visit:

www.brf.org.uk
www.brfonline.org.uk
www.barnabasinschools.org.uk
www.barnabasinchurches.org.uk
www.messychurch.org.uk
www.foundations21.org.uk

If you have any questions about BRF and our work, please email us at

enquiries@brf.org.uk